# Ned

## Autumn Music

## for Violin and Piano

Archive Edition

DISTRIBUTED BY

7777 W. BLUEMOUND RD. P.O. BOX 13819 MILWAUKEE, WI 53213

www.boosey.com
www.halleonard.com

Published by Boosey & Hawkes, Inc.
229 West 28th Street, 11th Fl
New York, NY 10001

www.boosey.com

*Commissioned by The Leonora Jackson McKim Fund in the Music Division, Library of Congress, and the International Violin Competition of Indianapolis, with a grant from the Payne Fund.*

# AUTUMN MUSIC

NED ROREM

2

# Ned Rorem

## Autumn Music

**Violin Part**

## for Violin and Piano

Archive Edition

7777 W. BLUEMOUND RD. P.O. BOX 13819 MILWAUKEE, WI 53213

www.boosey.com
www.halleonard.com

# AUTUMN MUSIC

**VIOLIN**

NED ROREM

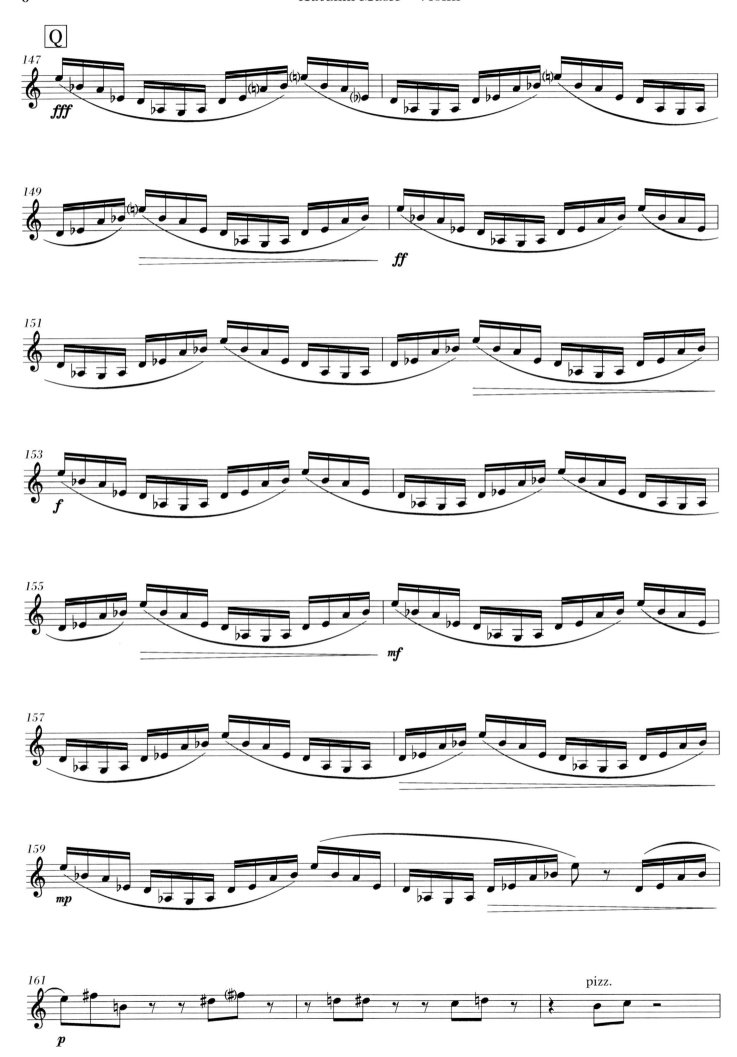

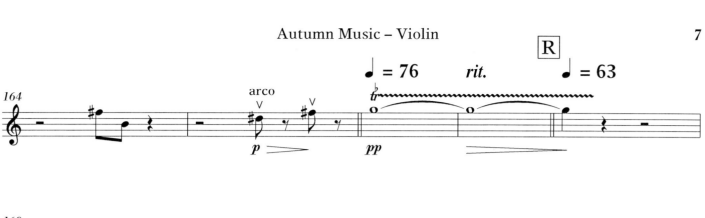

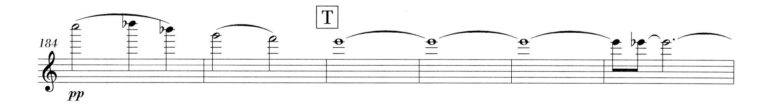

12

Nantucket/ New York
Autumn 1996